COPING WITH CHANGE

GAIL BROOKING

ISBN-13: 978-1512273113
ISBN-10: 1512273112

DEDICATION

To my parents, for teaching me the true value of life

CONTENTS

INTRODUCTION

I want to thank you for reading this book "Coping with Change' and hope that you enjoy it.

This book is a true, candid insight into the life of a miner who, having lived on the breadline, now finds herself in a world of excess. Is it about to change once more?

The distinction between the 'rich' and 'poor' is more evident than ever and you have to wonder who really has the better life. In addition, economic times are changing rapidly, with many people who have lived a life without worries about money finding changes on the horizon. Huge mortgages, no savings, and suddenly 'no job' for those who are not prepared will be met with much trepidation

CHAPTER 1

LIVING WITH LITTLE

"You might be poor, your shoes might be broken, but your mind is a palace. "

~ Frank McCourt

Growing up in the 50's and 60's was a beautiful experience. As a child, oblivious to what it took to keep our family fed and happy, "life was like a box of chocolates", as Forrest Gump would say.

Little did we know, most times there was not enough money to feed six children quality meals. Quite often, the smell of freshly baked bread and hot chocolate would grace our exquisitely set dinner table.

We had a happy childhood, with two devoted parents who loved us unconditionally. Lavish presents were non-existent. Living with little, did not matter to a young child who thought she had everything. Not once did I hear our parents say to us, 'we can't afford it.'

In the later years, we would learn that we were indeed very poor. That was surprising because, as I said, it seemed like we had everything. Although, coming home from school one day, a lot of furniture had mysteriously disappeared.

The age of innocence is a beautiful thing.

With money being scarce, our parents would often take us after school or on the weekends to work in the fields picking beans or tomatoes for extra money. We were not impressed, as you might imagine, but inadvertently it taught us how to work.

The 70's brought about a change for our family. My parents ended up with their own business and the work was a lot more lucrative for them.

However, 1971 would see a mighty change on the horizon.

Eighteen years old and newly married with a child and a few more to come, I learned very quickly what 'living with little' really meant.

My husband was a shearer, a back breaking job that relied heavily on the weather for our income. If it rained, there was no work and therefore, no money. Not having a regular pay each week took its toll. What did the word 'budget' mean? How do you bring up five children on an income that was very irregular?

Once, when our situation was pretty dire, we were advised to seek the help of a 'budget adviser'. In those days they took all your debt and wages, and only allotted us enough money for groceries and fuel. They had complete control, and worked with our creditors to reduce our debts.

Once all debt was paid down, we regained control of our budget. It was a great system except for one thing.

It did not educate us about how to handle our money. They simply took our problem away from us. Needless to say, it did not take long to return to our bad habits. We struggled on our own, too embarrassed to return to the 'budget advisor'

With very little money to go around you can guess which four words were constantly in my vocabulary, much to my regret, because my children grew up hearing it all the time: "we can't afford it".

Unfortunately today, those four words are spoken in the supermarket, and shopping malls, in fact everywhere you go. You see a child run to his mother asking if he could have something. You hear the mother telling her child, or in some cases actually screaming - "we can't afford it!" The reality of this scenario becomes more evident every day.

Of course there are exceptions. Money is not a concern for those who have it in abundance. Life has shown us that these circumstances can change and for many it does. The challenge is adjusting to it.

Robert Kiyosaki, the author *of Rich Dad, Poor Dad* constantly speaks about the lack of financial education in schools. He has been an advocate of change for many years and yet, for such a crucial subject, it still is not a priority for most educational systems. Imagine the impact it would have on future generations if it was.

Much later in life, my passion would turn to books, learning in general about life, how to be frugal, and how to manage money. I enjoyed studying the wealthy and how they lived.

Armed with all my newfound knowledge, my mother would also teach me a valuable lesson. "Knowledge is power," I said to her with a bit of arrogance. Her reply was, "knowledge has no power, unless you apply the action." She was right. You can have all the knowledge in the world and yet if you don't apply it - it means absolutely nothing.

Bruce Lee said "*knowing is not enough – you must apply. Willing is not enough – we must do.*"

It takes a lot of discipline to do that. The 3 D's: Determination, Dedication, and Discipline can be applied to every aspect of our lives. Making mistakes along the way has been a learning curve that has helped put perspective on coping with the hand that is dealt to us.

Some say it's harder for those who have experienced wealth, and when hard times hit or 'the bubble bursts' they are totally unprepared for what their life becomes. "Eat, drink, and be merry..." Living like there is no tomorrow will be the undoing of many in the economic times that await us.

CHAPTER 2

EAT, DRINK, AND BE MERRY...

"Two things help success in life: The way you manage when you have nothing. The way you behave when you have everything. "

~ Author unknown

I'm not sure which is worse, saying "we can't afford it" or "spend it like you've got it". Some things don't change. When you live from pay check to pay check, the mentality can easily become a 'what the heck' attitude, and so continues the vicious cycle of anxiously waiting for the next pay day.

The bills pile up and you simply ignore them. Unfortunately, they never go away. It becomes overwhelming, and you cover your ears when the phone rings or hide away when a creditor knocks on the door. They did that back in the 70's. Today with 'caller ID' it would be a lot easier to ignore them.

If I learned anything during my hard times with creditors, it was this: get up and face them head on. Ignoring them turned out to be a fatal mistake for me. Bankruptcy!

A lot of good comes out of adversity, although it's hard to recognize at the time. There is a huge stigma attached to bankruptcy but, in a way, it became our saving grace. It wasn't about losing the burden of debt, that's something we are not proud of. Credit became a trap because it was so easy to get. With credit no longer available to us for many years, we had no choice; we learned to live without it. This was to become a blessing in disguise.

Instant gratification, in most cases, is satisfied by **credit**. Who's laughing all the way to the bank? - **Creditors.** Who just walked in the door? **Interest.** I call it the '**Hangman's Noose**'. Why? Interest never sleeps, it's with you 24/7, never takes a vacation, is a noose around your neck, and will not die until you get rid of it.

Like ourselves in our early years, a lot of young people starting out in their career fall into this trap. They want it all now, the expensive cars, travel, and lifestyle. What of these things if the income stops?

The entertainment world is full of such people. They earn copious amounts of money, yet still use credit to buy houses and toys that exceed their incomes. The media is full of such stories about bankruptcy, caused by mindless spending.

Jane is in her 60's. She does not own a home. She has a lot of debt and is always avoiding the creditor's phone calls. She is a tireless worker with a huge spending habit. Her wardrobe is full of clothes that still have the tags on them from years ago. When you walk into her home, it is full of beautiful things everywhere.

What's amazing is her attitude towards money. She perfectly exemplifies the subject of this chapter: eat, drink, and be merry. Working in the mining industry, she earns a very good wage, but money does not faze her in the least. She simply enjoys spending every single dollar with no thought for tomorrow. "*I came into this world with nothing, and I will leave with nothing*," she told me once.

A single lady with no dependants, the world at her feet with respect to money, makes me wonder about the logic of it all. No savings, credit cards maxed out, and yet she can still smile. Asked how she coped with this way of living, she would simply shrug her shoulders and say, "*because I can.*"

Nicola has a similar attitude towards money. She's 44 with a big spending habit also. It is both puzzling and refreshing that money does not faze either of them. Nicola is very conscious of her commitments, pays everything on time, and then proceeds to spend the rest. Even if it leaves her with nothing till the next payday, she is happy.

Their circumstances are very similar. They are single, no dependants, many credit cards, and no savings. One earns twice as much as the other, yet they end up in the same boat, waiting with little money or none at all until pay day comes around again.

Like I said, what fascinates me about these two women is their attitude. Even though it is not the ideal way to live your life, they are both happy with nothing.

What if their circumstances changed? What if they both suddenly found themselves without a job and no immediate prospects of finding one? It would be a concern.

On the other hand, commitments and lack of money left me stressed and worried all the time. Don't get me wrong, there were a lot of highs as well. When the money came in there was no thought for the next week. Is there any real difference between us? Spending money until it was all gone, there was no difference. So in fact, my stress and worry was nothing more than a choice. It was self-inflicted. This would be my life for the next 36 years. It was all about to change.

One day, out of the blue, we got a call that would change the course of our lives. My husband was offered a job working in the mines. Can you imagine how we felt? We had no idea what an impact that phone call would have on our future.

On the 26th of January 2006, my husband flew out to the mines in West Australia. When he entered the mining industry we were heavily in debt, including a tax bill of $34,000

Overnight, my husband's wage went from a 5 figure income to a 6 figure income. For the first time in decades we were receiving a constant pay check that was more than we had ever seen. We paid our debts down very quickly. At long last we were finally 'debt free'. It's hard to explain one's feelings when you have lived with it for so long.

Securing a well-paid job as a pay officer, we now had two incomes and …….. you guessed it: we spent our money like there was no tomorrow. It felt amazing walking into the supermarket without sweating at the checkout. It felt good paying the phone bill on time. The change in our circumstances was like night and day, such a huge contrast.

We went from paying $450 per week in the city for our rental to $120 per MONTH for the home provided to us by the company. No power bills, no water bills. It was like going from rags to riches. That's a little extreme, but that's what it felt like.

Driving down the streets of our quaint little mining town, riches abounded. In the yards of many homes are caravans, four wheel drives, Harley Davidson bikes, boats everywhere. This may seem the norm for many, but when we first moved into town it was a sight to see.

It became endless. Shopping sprees, a Mediterranean cruise, designer bags, new cars, more travel, anything we wanted. At the end of the month there was very little left over, just like Jane and Nicola, except for one major difference. Our income was nearly four times higher and we had no bills, no credit cards, and no mortgage to pay and worse still – no savings.

We lived like this for four years, never thinking about tomorrow. We didn't save, we adopted the attitude of 'eat, drink, and be merry'

I like to think this life never changed who we are. We had become so de-sensitised to our surroundings that it's hard to keep a grip on reality. After all, there is a life outside these seemingly protected walls. It changes you, of this there is no doubt.

Is there a difference between those who have it all and those who don't? Where is the difference if you both live pay check- to- pay check? We may have more toys and the freedom to spend money, but if we have no savings or investments when we should have, then what makes us so different to those on less income who can't afford to save or invest?

Noel Whittaker wrote an excellent book called *Money Made Easy*, in the book he writes '*when your income goes up, so do your wants*.' In our case, that statement became true.

CHAPTER 3

TURNING OF THE TIDE

"The calm waters still the soul, allowing the influence of the divine to enter"

~ Gail Brooking

I don't know exactly when we came to our senses and stopped the shopping sprees, but we did. It was time to seriously contemplate the future. It didn't look bright, despite our income. What an utter waste just to appease our 'instant gratification'. We had nothing to show for all the money that we had earned over the past four years.

It was time to put all the knowledge learned about money management into practice. We set a goal to save for a deposit on a home. That sent a shiver up my spine for a moment. Here is why:

In 1989, still young and uneducated in the Australian economy, we built a home with no thought about the commitment we were up for. Our broker, after extensive searching found a credit union that was willing to give us a house loan. The 'big banks' thought we were too much of a risk.

No sooner had we moved into our dream home, the interest rates rose to a whopping 17%. Our dream was shattered practically overnight. We were in our home only eight months and we had to sell it or lose it. Going down that road again frightened me.

But the change in our circumstances saw us in a better position to become home owners again. We saved $40,000 – a huge amount in our eyes. Then house hunting began, and the excitement that came along with it. Things had certainly changed since the 80's. Prices were a lot higher than the $64k we paid back then and understandably so. Now the average price of a home was $350k. No matter, it's the way it is, and so the search for a good broker began.

Our first meeting with the broker started with the usual and then the subject of stamp duty came up. Our hard earned deposit was to be slashed in half because of 'stamp duty' and 'fees.' At that moment, the meeting was over for me. No one was going to get $20,000 of our hard earned money.

Deflation set in. We had holidays coming up in a few weeks. We would think about it after that.

We went to New Zealand for our yearly holiday at the beach, a welcome change from the red hot dirt that we work in. Being with family and friends is always a wonderful time to be had.

One day, we were sitting around the camp with my brother and his wife. We started discussing the housing market and I proceeded to tell him our experience. They are experts in this field. They had done very well over the years with 6 investment homes.

What I admire about this couple is that they are perfect examples of the 3 D's – dedication, discipline, and determination. Hard work and applied knowledge has rewarded them well. It never ceases to amaze me that it was achieved with good regular jobs, and a whole lot of wisdom.

We discussed what was happening in the Australian housing market. He looked at us very seriously and suggested that we look at purchasing an investment home in New Zealand. There was no stamp duty and the fees were very minimal. The homes were also a lot cheaper than Australia. His advice was sound. After all, we were in our fifties and to have a high mortgage at that time in our lives would have been suicide. He told us with the deposit we had there would be no problems securing a loan.

The very next day, the four of us left the beach and travelled down to his home town. He set up an appointment at the bank and the four of us went in and met the loans officer.

The loans officer was happy with our situation. Our income and deposit looked good on paper. There was one heart stopper for me in that meeting. She looked it all over and then informed us that, as foreign investors, we needed a 30% deposit. My first shock was being told we were foreigners in our own country. The second was hearing that we needed more money for the deposit. We barely had the 20%.

My husband, my sister-in-law, and I literally gave up in that moment. In fact, we actually stood up thinking it was all over. We were ready to leave with all hopes of owning a home at that time gone.

Lucky for us, my brother had more insight. He crossed his arms, looked the loans officer straight in the eyes, and with a defiant voice uttered these four words: *"what about the proposal?"*

To this day, I do not know what that meant, but the loans officer certainly did.   Within 24 hours we found a home, put an offer in, which was accepted, and secured the loan.

At long last we were homeowners again. That was January, 2010 – another major turning point in our lives.

CHAPTER 4

WHEN THE BUBBLE BURSTS

*"There are no guarantees in life. What we have today –
tomorrow can claim"*

~ Gail Brooking

In 2011, I was fortunate enough to secure a job alongside my husband in the mines driving trucks. This made our goal of owning our investment property outright very manageable.

With a lot of discipline, we managed to pay the home off in a little over a year. Then we had the idea to buy another investment home. We did, with the thought in mind that we would get the second home paid off quickly. After all, we had proved we could do it with the first one.

Unfortunately, we are human, and bad habits started to creep back into our lives slowly but surely. With the first home we were totally committed each and every month to become mortgage free. The second one took much longer; our commitment and discipline were not as intense as with the first home. It shows that sometimes old habits take a long time to die, if at all.

We eventually did get it paid, by selling the first one. Our goal was to buy cheap, sell, and upgrade to a better home, which we did. We used this same strategy to procure our third property, our retirement home. Selling the second home, we put the proceeds on to our third property and paid it off.

We are now mortgage free, have a beautiful home with 2 acres, lots of fruit trees, and did it all in the 5 years, - as we had planned.

We have been riding the mining boom since we entered the industry in 2006. There are many people that have been here over 30 years who have seen both good and bad times in the mines. All in all, life has blessed them beyond people's imagination.

Not long after we moved to town, a conversation with an acquaintance astounded me. She informed me that she lived from pay check to pay check and most months would have hardly any money left in the bank. It was hard to imagine that with such a good income, there were people living like that. As you know, it didn't take me long to fall into that category.

It's easy to take things we have for granted. Living inside our bubble, we tend to forget that once we had nothing. That world as we knew it, far removed from our minds. It is fair to say that one day it could all be taken from us.

A couple of years ago my husband said a strange thing to me. He told me that what happened to the wool industry a few years back would happen to the mining industry. *"Mark my words,"* he said. *"It might take a couple of years, but it will happen."* His prediction was spot on, almost to the day. It's a bit uncanny, because he said the same thing about the wool industry well before it happened.

Moving forward to 2015, the mining industry is in turmoil. For many people the bubble has already burst and they are worried. The price of ore per tonne has fallen dramatically, especially in the last few months. It seems to be in free fall.

In January 2014 the iron ore price was $134 per tonne. As of today it is $58 per tonne with predictions that it could fall even more. It does not take a genius to see the writing on the wall. The simple math tells us what is happening, or is about to happen.

Were there many that saw this a year ago? Did any of us predict that we could possibly lose our six-figure income? For many, it has happened already.

The changes we have seen over the last few weeks have been cold and swift, forcing smaller mines to shut their doors. As recently as last week, 600 people lost their jobs from one mine.

We are not the only industry that is feeling the pinch. What's happening out in the world is having a profound effect across all sectors.

For a couple of years now, as the state of the world declines, there have been signs that have many people worried about their future.

A prominent economist who I listen to regularly frightened me with his predictions. Taking what he said very seriously, I made a commitment to come up with an exit strategy and make preparations as quickly as possible. This was over a year ago, well before our industry reached the point it is at today.

He speaks of tough times ahead for all of us. He predicted Japans recession of 1990-1992 and the 2008 credit crisis and stock market crash. He now predicts that an even greater crash is coming, and he is not the only one saying that. If you want to know what's really happening out there, follow the money. In other words, watch what the wealthy are doing today.

It worries me that our children and grandchildren will feel the effects more greatly than we do. Preparing and making them aware that a global crisis is on the horizon is imperative. Evidence is beginning to appear and at a speed that is quite devastating. The last thing we need right now is to read all the doom and gloom out there. At the same time, we can't put our head in the sand and pretend it's not happening thinking that nothing is going to change.

We all know that is not true: change is inevitable.

CHAPTER 5

COPING WITH CHANGE

"Do not be afraid of change - it is leading you to a new beginning"

~ Author unknown

If you study the way wealthy people invest, you'll see they never do it without an exit strategy. You don't have to be wealthy to do this: the only requirement, as Nike says is, - *"Just Do It"* -.

There is a beautiful quote from Reinhold Niebuhr: *"God grant me the serenity to accept the things I cannot change, the courage to change the things I can, and the wisdom to know the difference."*

Life throws us many curve balls. Change in circumstance, especially if we don't see it coming, can be very overwhelming.

Recently, a good friend of ours lost his mining job. It was totally unexpected and he didn't see it coming. He was devastated and it took him a few days to tell his wife. He was not afraid of her reaction, but the effect that it was going to have on their lives. They had a high mortgage, debt and two children in boarding school.

Getting on in age and with the mining industry in a mess, he had no idea what he was going to do. He knew that if he couldn't find something quickly, the first thing that would go would be his home.

Sometimes we sit in our glass houses watching the world go by with no concern for what is happening out there in the real world. It is only when it has an impact on our own lives that we sit up and take notice, but by then it may be too late.

Safety is a major concern in our industry to the point that it has top priority over production. We are constantly on the lookout for hazards that are detrimental to our safety which, if found, are reported instantly no matter how small or insignificant we may think it is. When identified, changes are made immediately to keep us safe. It's basically being aware all the time of what is happening around you.

We can apply that to our lives by being aware of changes both in our own environment and in the world. Believe it or not what is happening out there, especially in the USA, affects us here in Australia in one way or another. There are many hazards out there that could ultimately be our downfall if we are not prepared.

There is a lot to be said for a lifetime of experiences. You tend to accumulate such experience by the time you reach your sixties.

Each of our circumstances may be different but the principle remains the same. I know of no educational system out there that can teach me how to cope with change better than life itself. Life's lessons are all around.

Taking notice and being able to *"accept the things I cannot change"*- learning to face changes is how we coped with a lot of adversity in our lives. I am a strong advocate for a positive attitude now, it's crucial. Moping never helped me or anyone.

There is nothing more traumatic for a mother than to lose one of her children. It was a day before my thirty second birthday when our fifth child was born. Our beautiful son, had the most glorious head of pitch black hair, what a joyous occasion it was. Being a caesarean birth, I awoke in recovery all alone. Our son was not in the room, which was odd. Not long afterwards a doctor came in, as cold as ice he told me that our son would not last a month. Given the condition he had, there were only six known cases and all of those children died within their first 30 days.

There I was, alone in a cold hospital room with the news that our son would not live. To this day I will never understand why the doctor could not wait for my husband to be by my side, before he gave me that devastating news. Our son would be with us for only two more days.

The following weeks after his passing, depression set in. It felt like living without existing. Tears would fall a lot, especially when I was alone. A special friend of mine recognized the signs. She had lost her son in an accident a few years back. She taught me some valuable lessons about how to accept what had happened. She reminded me that I had four other beautiful children and a loving husband that needed me more than ever.

Our son will never be far from our minds and learning to, "*accept the things we cannot change*" - became a valuable lesson to me.

It never ceases to amaze me how many positive things are around us. They certainly outweigh the negatives.

In this beautiful land of Australia we are blessed with so much. Despite what the world may think (doom and gloom, etc.) it is still a land of great opportunities and new beginnings. Einstein said, "*in the middle of difficulty lies opportunity*."

Gratitude has an amazing effect. Reading the book '*The Secret*' helped me learn to be grateful for the smallest thing. The food we are privileged to have in such abundance is just one. There are many in the world who have very little of this most basic need.

Moving forward with a grateful heart, a positive mind, and an unbeatable attitude is a beautiful recipe for a happier life.

CHAPTER 6

MOVING FORWARD

"If you believe you can accomplish everything by "cramming" at the eleventh hour, by all means, don't lift a finger now. But you may think twice about beginning to build your ark once it has already started raining"

~ Max Brooks

With the threat of unemployment hanging over our industry, or any other for that matter, preparation has become imperative.

Our company is very generous to its employees. With so many perks available, to think about living without them is daunting to say the least. But reality tells me that one day this will all be over, whether that is through retirement or being laid off from the job.

I am under no illusion that we could lose our jobs tomorrow for whatever reason, be it economic or otherwise. If we don't have our preparations in place, we will more than likely find ourselves back where we started.

On the verge of retirement, looking back at our lives, we were given a second chance. We do not take it lightly. We are very lucky that we have a free hold

23

home, savings, and the superannuation to look forward to. But is it enough?

To be honest, it probably isn't, if you believe what the experts tell you. What they don't know is that living with little is not new to us. If we had to do it again, we could, only this time with a lot more knowledge and wisdom.

As part of my plan, I looked at the worst possible scenario. No savings and only the pension to rely on. Finding out the rates for a pensioner couple, I did a month's trial living on $500 a week. To say it was tough was an understatement.

It made me realize how wasteful I was. How much we take for granted, how we buy unnecessary things. It was the most soul- searching experiment I have ever done and opened my eyes tremendously. Had we forgotten where we had come from?

I made a conscious decision to learn all about being self-sufficient. It was part of my 'exit strategy.'

YouTube became my newfound friend. Soaking up all the knowledge, my home became a busy little beehive, making soap powders, cleaning products, jams and chutneys, even my own butter. It was exciting and very fulfilling. It would serve its purpose for our future when the income stops.

Shopping for groceries has changed. This question follows me down every shopping aisle, *"do we really need that?"* It works; it's like having a little friend tapping you on the shoulder and saying, "*no.*" Since implementing that simple question, our grocery bill is a lot cheaper. It sounds like a cliché but doing a menu plan and shopping to it really does save money.

Changing my spending habits became a priority, keeping it as close as possible to the life we are about to embark on and the life that we once knew many years ago. Making these changes is very important as we come to terms with letting go of this opulent life. Maybe our transition will be a lot easier because we have prepared.

What helped me come to my senses and actually put this plan in place was my sister. She lived in Perth until a year ago, and then circumstances saw her move back to New Zealand permanently. Before she left, she had a good income. Like me she would spend her wages on whatever she wanted without ever having to say, "I can't afford it."

Now, when I call her on the phone, those four words have become a part of her life. She literally cannot afford any luxuries in any form. Together we worked out her finances so she could cope with her newfound situation.

It was such a dramatic change for her. She literally went from being a '*have*' to a '*have not*'. Those are not my words; some man said that of the human race. "*There are only the haves the have nots*" In a sense it is true - but only where money is concerned.

The one thing I can say is that the change has made her a better person. She is very humble and has accepted the things she cannot change with dignity. She has learned to be so self-sufficient it puts me to shame. To live on less than $500 a week and expect that to cover all expenses is doing it really tough.

Even though money is scarce, she told me she would not trade the life she has now for the life she had in Perth. There is a quality of life she enjoys that no amount of money can buy. Peace. I believe she is one of the '*haves.*'

Food storage is a huge priority in our home. Our church has always advocated the need to have at least three months' supply of food and enough finances to cover all expenses for those three months as well.

Losing a job can be devastating, having no emergency funds even more so. Implementing this one simple plan will give us security and peace of mind.

You can prevent a crisis in your life today, by simply taking action.

Chapter 7

Believing

"Lots of people limit their possibilities by giving up easily. Never tell yourself this is too much for me. It's no use, I can't go on. If you do, you are licked by your own thinking. Keep believing and keep on keeping on."

~ Norman Vincent Peale

I read a book recently that has worked wonders for many people. It's available on Kindle and is called, It Works. It's a very short story, but it is packed with a simple solution about how to achieve what we want.

It's a very simplified version of *The Secret.*

There will be a few sceptics out there about this method of achievement. The number of people who have changed their lives using it is astonishing, and in my opinion far outweigh the sceptics. Personal experience has seen this method work both positively and negatively for me. There is so much power generated from the thoughts we convey.

Remaining positive in adversity certainly is not easy. It takes a lot of willpower to rid your brain of these negative thoughts. Your brain knows no difference, only what you tell it.

A few years back, a job became available that I wanted. Having no experience at all in the field, I went ahead and submitted an application. Putting the method of *The Secret* into practice, in my own mind I already had the job.

On an index card these were the words that I repeated in my head over and over again all day every day. "*I work for ....and I am the best employee they have ever had in that position.*"

It was said with such conviction I ended up believing it was already mine. Needless to say, that statement became true.

It can have an adverse effect as well.

My weight was stagnant and had been for a long time. It was time to do something about it. Using the method that had worked so well for that job, it seemed like a good idea to try it for weight loss.

On my card and in my head these words were repeated: "*I am drastically losing weight no* matter *what I eat*"........ The weight dropped off me very quickly and **drastically** with a devastating effect on my health. I became very ill.

Look at the word that was being repeated over and over again, **drastically**. The dictionary defines it as **extremely severe; radical**

The word 'healthy' should have replaced 'drastically' this shows how it can work against you if you're not careful.

Muhammad Ali, some say, was the greatest boxer who ever lived. He would annoy me with his arrogance when he called himself '*the greatest*'. He was such a show off, constantly telling the world he was the best. It wasn't until he finished his career that it became clear to me that he was not arrogant, he just believed.

On my wall is a magnificent picture of Muhammad Ali and Michael Jordon together and the heading is titled, "*The Greatest*". He would never have achieved that goal if he did not first believe that he was great to begin with.

What you tell yourself everyday will either lift you up or tear you down.

No one is exempt from challenges. Challenges acknowledge no distinction between class, race, or religion. They come when you least expect it and in many different forms, be it health, finances, death, unemployment, or depression. The list is extensive.

What do you think happens when all you say is:

"*I can't get a job*" or "*I can't afford it*"? If we keep saying things like this, they will manifest quicker than we can say 'Jack Robinson'.

Happiness is a choice, circumstances may affect it, but you're still the one who decides your happiness. Author unknown

CHAPTER 8

REALITY

"How reluctantly the mind consents to reality."

~ Norman Douglas

Retirement and reality are on my doorstep. There will be a season of change once more. In a few months, life as we know it will be over. Taking a look at this roller coaster ride, the picture becomes clear. It seems almost crude to try to sum it up in one sentence.

We have lived below the breadline, we have lived with excess, and the near future will see us once again living a more frugal life.

There is a difference between being poor and being frugal, they are not the same thing. As harsh as it may sound, living poor is a choice. Nelson Mandela said this: *"poverty is not an accident, like slavery and apartheid. It is man-made and can be removed by the actions of human beings"*.

There are many inspiring stories of people who live below the breadline, yet are living a good life because of the choices they make - discipline is their friend.

Making bad choices kept us on the breadline. We were not frugal, we did not think ahead, nor did we give up things that we should have. If we had, then stress would not have found itself in our home.

Looking back at my life, my thoughts reflect upon the fortunes we have been blessed with. In the end we can have it all, but it will never replace the values that were taught to me as a child. We had a warm home, food on the table, and the love of our parents. I had forgotten how priceless these simple things are, and how easy it is to take them for granted.

When my siblings and I left home to venture into the big wide world, all we had were the values and teachings our parents gave us. What we did with them was entirely up to us. The day we left was the moment we each began to shape our own futures. As it is with humans, we all ended up with very diverse outcomes.

A beautiful quote I love from Pres. David O McKay says. "*No other success can compensate for failure in the home.*" There is a lot to be said for teaching our children to appreciate the simple things, ensuring that when they leave our care, the values we have taught them, will be a solid grounding for their own future.

Lessons are learned along this highway we call 'life'. To live it with trepidation would find us missing things not seen, simply because we were not looking.

As the twilight of change awaits me, I find myself looking for the new dawn, peace filling my heart knowing that what the future holds is yet another chapter to be lived. When the income stops, there is peace in knowing that our preparation for this change has been established.

.... *"It's easy to forget what an amazing gift life really is. Our lives are but a blink, yet for one brief moment we get to experience the wonders of our existence"*..........